POSH PROTOCOL
Volume II

~

BEING PRESIDENTIAL

POSH PROTOCOL Volume II

~

BEING PRESIDENTIAL

C. C. Preston • Dr. Posh ®

Copyright © 2019

Copyright © 2019 C.C. Preston, Dr. Posh®
All rights reserved. Author Photos Purchased. Printed in the United States. No part of this book may be used or reproduced in any form or manner without written permission, except in the case of brief quotations embodied in articles and reviews.

ISBN 10: 0-578-58240-6
ISBN 13: 978-0-578-58240-5

TO

The Holy Spirit,

I Love You

CONTENTS

Being Presidential
Defined — 1

Being Presidential
A Cognitive System — 5

Being Presidential
A Call To Action — 11

Being Presidential
A Way of Life — 15

Being Presidential
Building Your Fuchsia Force™ — 19

Being Presidential
Enter Your Own Room & Build Your Own Table — 23

Being Presidential
A Global Outreach — 27

CONTENTS

Being Presidential
The Monetization Process — 31

Being Presidential
Managing Financial Success — 35

Being Presidential
Managing Social Media — 39

Being Presidential
Implementing Self-Care — 43

Being Presidential
Birthing New Presidents — 47

Prayer of Salvation — 55

ACKNOWLEDGMENTS

Giving Honor and Thanks to my
Lord and Savior Jesus Christ.
I am nothing without God.

Presidential Prayer

Abba Father,
Endow us with the knowledge, wisdom and power to always be a Presidential Representation of You.

We Love You, Always.

In the Name of Jesus, Amen

"But ye shall receive power, after that the Holy Ghost is come upon you. . ."
(Acts 1:8, King James Version)

Being Presidential

Defined

The term Presidential simply means the "nature of a President." [1] A President is "a person who presides."[2] To preside means "to exercise management or control." [3] Being Presidential means managing the gift of life and all other God given gifts, talents and assignments while exercising control through faith. Being Presidential requires Presidential Cognition, as well as the ability to take quick action. It also requires you to embrace a new way of living, a new way of life.

Being Presidential means speaking the language of a President. As Presidents we Speak Fuchsia™, the language of women in leadership. Being Presidential necessitates building a Fuchsia Force™ perhaps even while constructing your own speaking platform from start to finish. It requires global outreach with implemented monetization of your products and services.

Being Presidential encompasses Leadership. Leadership is the act of leading, guiding or directing.[4] You must take the lead in managing your financial success. This means being present to make important financial decisions and reviewing financial documents for accuracy.

Being Presidential means being an effective Social Media Manager or delegating this responsibility accordingly. Being a President means taking responsibility for implementing self-care. With all that is going on around you, do not get lost in your accomplishments. Stop, relax and indulge in self-care.

One of the greatest responsibilities of a President is assisting with the birth of a new President. Speak life, hope and growth into the lives of others. Teach them how to operate in their own unique gifts and talents. Your reward for this will be great through Christ Jesus.

Being Presidential

A Cognitive System

The key to developing a Presidential Cognitive System is to develop the mind of Christ. Our biblical text tells us ". . .be not conformed to this world: but be ye transformed by the renewing of your mind, that ye may prove what is that good, and acceptable, and perfect, will of God." (Romans 12:2 KJV)

Cognition is "the act or process of knowing; "[5] It is also our perception.[5] How we perceive ourselves and our environment will shape our views and decisions. If our mind is focused on Christ, we will have a Godly perception of ourselves and begin to know ourselves as leaders through the eyes of Christ. This then becomes the foundational focal point of developing a Presidential Cognitive System, which is the system of perceiving and knowing that God has created us to be managers and leaders over our own lives and over the gifts and talents he has bestowed upon us.

Our Presidential Cognitive System needs continual nurturing and expansion. There are numerous ways to feed this system. Most importantly pray and ask God to enlarge this area of your life. Use your heavenly language to commune with the Holy Spirit.

When fortifying your Presidential Cognitive System seek out sources of knowledge on the topics of management and leadership. Read biographies about successful leaders with Godly character and integrity. You must "study to shew thyself approved unto God, a workman that needeth not to be ashamed, rightly dividing the word of truth." (2 Timothy 2:15 KJV)

Attend conferences and symposiums hosted by your local church and those hosted globally by successful Christian leaders. Godly character will be birthed in you in these environments.

It is

Time

To Make Some

Executive Decisions

Being Presidential

A Call To Action

You are hereby activated! You are a President! You preside over your life and the gifts and talents God has given you. Go, move, take action! Operate in the personification of a President. Serve, lead, guide, build, manage, create, give, develop and teach others to be great leaders and great Presidents.

Hello Madam President™ embrace your position. Nurture & feed your Presidential character. Make an Executive Decision to be bold, effective, shrewd, positive and powerful. Stand in your own stilettos with courage and know that " . . . he which hath begun a good work in you will perform it until the day of Jesus Christ." (Philippians 1:6 KJV)

Make an Executive Decision to be extraordinary and change the world, as we know it. Implement new protocols as an active President. You will succeed, grow, flourish, prevail, thrive and win!

Think big, stand tall and Don Your Diadem™. Do not recoil, retreat or reduce your size to make others feel comfortable in your presence. Dominate your space and walk in the dominion and authority God has given you. Know without a doubt that you are a President. Know that you belong in the room and at the table where world-changing ideas are being exchanged and world-changing decisions are being made.

Make an Executive Decision and invest in your perpetual growth and development as a leader, as a President. Those who will follow your lead deserve your best self. Cultivate a hunger and a yearning for knowledge and wisdom.

Remember to guard your heart, as not everyone will be receptive of your position as President. Some may blatantly express this, others may feign support while secretly opposing you. Be vigilant and be on guard!

Being Presidential

A Way Of Life

There is an opportunity to be Presidential in every facet of life. Being Presidential is a permanent transformation. Your Presidential position is an ongoing post that does not expire. Being Presidential should permeate the very fiber of your being. This is not something you put on and then take off. Being Presidential is who you are, not just what you do.

You are a President when you are alone and when the whole world is watching. You are a President when you are speaking to one person and when you are speaking to millions. You are a President as a Mother, Daughter, Sister or Friend. Your name carries the position of President. You are a President whether others recognize you as such or not.

Hello Madam President™ we've been waiting for you to show up and do what you do. We've been waiting for you to show up and speak Gods truths through his living word.

The Heart of a President is Fuchsia™ and as Presidents we speak from our heart. We Speak Fuchsia™! Fuchsia is the positive, powerful, edifying language of Women in Leadership. Wherever your feet may tread as you walk through life, speak wisdom, hope and revitalization into those under the sound of your voice. Speak Fuchsia™!

As a President, as a leader your responsibility is greater *but* so is your reward! "Trust in the Lord with all thine heart; and lean not unto thine own understanding. In all thy ways acknowledge him, and he shall direct thy paths." (Proverbs 3:5-6 KJV)

Being Presidential is a way of life. It is a lifestyle. You are a President while cooking dinner and doing laundry. You are a President during seed time and harvest. You are a President now and forever. You will always be a President in the eyes of God.

Being Presidential

Building Your Fuchsia Force™

Your Fuchsia Force™ is your close circle of business confidants and friends. This is a specialized group of people that bring you encouragement and praise. You can trust them with business matters and personal matters. Your Fuchsia Force™ reminds you of the thoughts that God has toward you and the plans he has for your life. They bring you opportunities for advancement that you may not have been aware of. They instruct you in ways to bring yourself closer to the Lord.

Your Fuchsia Force™ wants to see you succeed and grow as a President. When building your Force, it is essential that you ask God to evaluate the person and reveal their true intentions. Use your God given discernment to determine if the person is truly for you or against you. People who are for you will always lead you toward the word of God, for there is life in Gods word.

When building your Fuchsia Force™ choose like-minded people who have interests similar to yours. Choose people who love the Lord and enjoy some of the same activities as you do. Choose people to join your Force that will tell you no and will extend to you brutally honest counsel when you are making life-changing Presidential decisions.

Your Fuchsia Force™ is with you through seed time and harvest. These are the people who are not just with you when everything is going well. Your Force stays with you through disappointment and heartache. Your Force encourages you during your recovery process.

Your Fuchsia Force™ does not remain silent when others speak of you negatively in their presence. They make it clear that they are aligned with who you are and who you represent. When people see your Force they should know they represent Christ.

Being Presidential

Enter Your Own Room & Build Your Own Table

As a President you will be required to be a pioneer. You will at times be the first to do thing or the first to do it the way that you are doing it. Not everyone will be enthusiastic or overjoyed about doing something new or innovative. Change can sometimes be challenging for people. So understand everyone will not be waiting to embrace you due to the words that are coming out of your mouth.

You may have to enter your own room and build your own table. In other words, you may have to book your own venue, host your own event, stand on the platform that you have created and deliver your message. You may not always get that invitation to come and deliver a message on someone else's platform. Be prepared to create your own. View this as a unique opportunity to have direct creative control over the platform you will be presenting on.

Know that you are called to be a President to build something new, exciting, demanding and challenging. You are called to the front to be an example to those who will follow your lead. You are called to have a positive impact on those who hear your voice and observe your actions. By entering your own room and building your own table you have set the stage for another arena through which you can pass the baton to the next leader being built.

Building your own platform with the help of the Holy Spirit gives rise to the opportunity to connect with other platforms that are being built at the same level and pace as yours. Rise to the occasion and spring forth as the pioneer that you are. As a President be emboldened with tenacity and courage to accomplish your mission and achieve your goals. "In every thing give thanks: for this is the will of God in Christ Jesus concerning you."
(1 Thessalonians 5:18 KJV)

Being Presidential

A Global Outreach

As a President it is important to know as much about your intended audience as possible so that your message is as effective as possible. Some information that you disseminate will be created and intended for a specific audience. Perhaps a specific audience within your local community, however there should be parts of that message that are applicable to other people in other places in the world, as we are all interconnected.

Hello Madam President™ you've been called to the Nations. Your gift, your message and your leadership are needed globally. Your message is for the world. There may be cultural barriers, language barriers and distance barriers, however your message is still one for the planet. Give your message to the world. We each need our global community to grow, glean, glisten and become greater. We are all Gods children joined to one body in Christ.

As a President, it is your responsibility to travel the globe and learn about different cultures. Visit as many countries as possible by setting a goal each year to visit a specific number of countries. To prepare for your trips, study and learn about the people, the cuisine, the churches and the architectural landmarks. Remember to be kind, generous and gracious to the local community in the country you are visiting.

Build your network and establish Presidential connections while you are traveling abroad. Please do not expect everyone in other countries to be just like the people in your home country. Our diversity is what makes us rich and intriguing. As you travel near and far incorporate what you have learned into your leadership style and your message. Through prayer, ask God to expand the borders of your mind and increase your knowledge of the cultural values of others.

Being Presidential

The Monetization Process

Hello Madam President™ you are your own unique brand. Every woman is her own brand. Your brand is your personal distinguishable style that represents who you are. Your brand may consist of your name, your logo, your signature color and many other items that uniquely represent you and how you operate as a President.

It is your time and your season to prosper! As a President, you have an obligation to determine which of the principles, practices and strategies you are currently using can be monetized for the benefit of the Kingdom by being offered in the marketplace. Put pen to paper and write your next book, keynote speech or blog.

Ask yourself the right questions. Is your book suitable for e-book publication *and* paper publication? Is your keynote speaking honorarium at the market rate for the city and state in which your will be speaking? Is your blog producing income?

As you evaluate what is already in your hand you will find ways to monetize your gifts and your leadership abilities. As a President, this too is under the umbrella of your responsibility. Ask yourself, is there perhaps a new product that can be created for the marketplace within your brand?

Perhaps your speaking skills will perform well in a regularly scheduled webinar or seminar setting in addition to your keynote-speaking platform. You may offer your knowledge at the current market rate through an abundance of online teaching platforms.

Be prepared to take those in your audience to their next level of growth by offering a product or service that takes them beyond the boundaries of their current knowledge base. It is important to keep the momentum of learning new information moving forward toward the future.

Being Presidential

Managing Financial Success

There is a process to successfully managing your success. We often express our desire for wealth and success, however there seems to be much less dialog about how to manage that wealth and success when it does manifest. Are you prepared to pay $250,000 per month in tithes to the church of which you are a member? This is merely 10% of a monthly income of $2.5 million.

Are you prepared to file and pay quarterly taxes to the IRS when required by law? Are you prepared to hire an Accountant and have and Attorney on retainer at all times? You will most likely need a full team of professionals to manage a sizable amount of wealth. These are just of few of the questions you should ask yourself regarding the successful management of your success. As a President this is an area where being proactive is a must. Safeguarding your financial holdings is essential.

Does your current home that you reside in produce income along with your other real estate holdings? Is your wealth being properly invested in income producing assets? Or are you squandering your wealth by being more of a consumer than an investor? Is your wealth producing income in multiple countries, in multiple currencies? Are you reviewing your own financial statements and bank accounts for accuracy *after* your team has reviewed them? Who besides you can sign documents on your behalf and is having a second signer necessary?

Are you building generational wealth or are you nouveau riche? Are you building your legacy and your future or are you purchasing the latest flashy trends? Have definitive answers to these questions by knowing and understanding the process of successfully managing your success. Engage in wealth preservation instead of wealth depletion.

Being Presidential

Managing Social Media

Determine which social media platforms are well suited for your objectives and your brand. Once you have established this, create a social media strategy for how to accomplish the goals you have set for your social media success.

Is your objective to grow your audience, disseminate information or sell products and services? Perhaps it is a combination of all of these things. After confirming which platform is better for which task, set a schedule of how many posts per platform per day, per week, etc. Spend some time researching and learning the tools that are available, such as hashtags.

As a President, you will see the importance of identifying the current market trends as it relates to social media. What are the headlines this week and how do they relate to my message and my brand? What are the trending hashtags and how can I incorporate them in my message?

In addition, as a pioneer you will create your own hashtags and topic headlines for your message and your brand. As a President, know that your speaking topics will evolve over time, however your core message is the same – Christ Over Everything!

As your spirit becomes stronger, through the Holy Spirit, your message will become stronger. We know that the Holy Spirit endows us with power as taught to us in Act 1:8 "But ye shall receive power, after that the Holy Ghost is come upon you: and ye shall be witnesses unto me …"

If you have received the indwelling of the Holy Spirit with the evidence of speaking in tongues, use your heavenly language to converse with the Holy Spirit. Ask the Holy Spirit to guide all your thoughts and guide all your ways. Know, grow and lead through the Holy Spirit. He will give you your Presidential voice and your Presidential message.

Being Presidential

Implementing Self-Care

Self-care is the best care. Rest, recuperate and rejuvenate. A large portion of self-care involves exercising, consuming nutritional meals and getting an adequate amount of sleep. Do not become so consumed with your Presidential mission that you fail to properly care for yourself. The most important self-care behaviors include reading the word of God daily, praying and using your heavenly language to commune with the Holy Spirit. Submit your request for spiritual rest and relaxation to God.

Grab hold of your rest and peace. This may require dismissing toxic personalities from your personal space. Being in close proximity to these kinds of personalities is draining. Release disturbances like this from your life. Protect your peace and cherish it. Give help and assistance when possible but do not allow yourself to get pulled into a negative downward spiral of circumstances.

Conduct research on your local spas. Be proactive in your search for ways to indulge in self-care. Search for international spas and resorts in countries you frequent or plan to visit in the future. Read published reviews and recommendations from former and current spa patrons. If the spa that you plan to visit has had any governmental health code violations, please reconsider your choice.

Visit the spa of your choice often and freely indulge in the services offered by the spa, including facials, full body massage, eyebrow shaping, manicures and pedicures. You may receive your spa services in silence, or while listening to Christian music, jazz or spa music. Relax, relax, relax and then relax! Put you mobile phone away, and focus on the goodness of the Lord. Recite and remember, "the Lord is my strength and my shield; my heart trusted in him, and I am helped…" (Psalm 28:7 KJV)

Being Presidential

Birthing New Presidents

As a President, your leadership DNA must be traceable in the lives of those who will lead after you. One of the key responsibilities of any great leader is birthing new leaders. While operating in your gifts, you must teach others how to walk in and operate in their own gifts. It is a birthing process for you and for them. You are birthing a new President through your gifts and they are birthing a new President (themselves) by bringing forth their gifts.

Passing the baton of leadership is merely one way in which we as Presidents can be good stewards with the gifts God has given us. This is the will of God as told to us in 1 Peter 4:10 KJV "As every man hath received the gift, even so minister the same one to another, as good stewards of the manifold grace of God." We are blessed so that we may be a blessing to someone else. Sharing our gifts with others is how our gifts are multiplied.

As with other birthing processes, birthing new Presidents can be labor intensive. Sometimes the one who is being birthed does not understand everything that is happening during the birthing process. They may not understand until after the process is complete. As a President, as a leader, you will need patience, perseverance and endurance during this time. Continue to pour into them and expect excellence out of them.

This birthing process takes time and may require you to travail. This is the time to be in constant conversation with the Holy Spirit so that you may be instructed in the correct teaching methods and strategies.

As a President, your labor and generosity will be rewarded. God sees your good works and the paths that you take, as it is written in Job 23:10 KJV " But he knoweth the way that I take: when he hath tried me, I shall come forth as gold."

CONCLUSION

POSH PROTOCOL Volume II BEING PRESIDENTIAL is Your Go-To Guide for being a Presidential Representation of Christ. Adopt and embrace a Presidential Cognitive System and then take prompt action. Being Presidential is a way of life. It is not just what you do, it is who you are.

Build your Fuchsia Force™ with caution and discernment. Speak Fuchsia™ on your own speaking platform and on global stages. Monetize your successes and manage your successes properly. Do not forget to rest and take care of yourself. Finally, pass your gifts along to others so that they too can be great Presidents.

~~~

Most importantly, if you would like to accept Jesus Christ as your personal Savior, *simply turn the page,* believe and pray the prayer of Salvation.

> *"...if thou shalt confess with thy mouth the Lord Jesus, and shalt believe in thine heart that God raised him from the dead, thou shalt be saved."*

Romans 10:9

Prayer of Salvation

Heavenly Father,
I confess I am a sinner. I repent of my sins. I believe your son Jesus Christ died for my sins. He was raised from the dead and He is alive right now. I accept Jesus Christ as my Lord and Savior now and forever. Lord, I surrender my life to you completely. Holy Spirit dwell within me and manifest your presence within me through an impartation of my own spoken heavenly language.

Amen

Disclaimer

While the author and publisher have used their best efforts in preparing this book, they make no representations with respect to the accuracy or completeness of the contents of this book and specifically disclaim any implied warranties.

The material contained herein is for general information purposes. The author, publisher and all affiliates accept no responsibility and exclude all liability in connection with the use or application of the information contained herein. Words or phrases followed by the trademark symbol (™) are the trademarked property of the author.

The brand name Dr. Posh® does not denote a doctoral or medical degree. The brand name Dr. Posh® is connotative of C.C. Preston's competence in Posh Protocol, Etiquette and Advocacy.

References

1. Presidential. (n.d.). *Online Dictionary.* Retrieved September 9, 2019, from http://dictionary.com/browse/presidential
2. President. (n.d.). *Online Dictionary.* Retrieved September 9, 2019, from http://dictionary.com/browse/president
3. Preside. (n.d.). *Online Dictionary.* Retrieved September 9, 2019, from http://dictionary.com/browse/preside
4. Leadership. (n.d.). *Online Dictionary.* Retrieved September 9, 2019, from http://dictionary.com/browse/leadership
5. Cognition. (n.d.). *Online Dictionary.* Retrieved September 9, 2019, from http://dictionary.com/browse/cognition

The Holy Bible, King James Version

ABOUT THE AUTHOR

C.C. Preston, branded as **Dr. Posh®** is the Posh Protocol Specialist – The Nation's Only Etiquettician® [Edə, ket, tiSHən]

C.C. Preston, Dr. Posh® is a woman after God's own heart. The Speaker and Entrepreneur is also the author of Posh Protocol Volume I The Ten Commandments of Christian Accouterment for Women.

All the Glory belongs to God!

www.ingramcontent.com/pod-product-compliance
Lightning Source LLC
LaVergne TN
LVHW051209080426
835512LV00019B/3181